Garfield
Says It With Flowers

JIM DAVIS

RAVETTE PUBLISHING

© 1993 United Feature Syndicate, Inc.

© 1993 United Feature Syndicate, Inc.

JIM DAVIS 6-18

© 1993 United Feature Syndicate, Inc.

DON'T YOU HATE THOSE LITTLE CRUMBS THAT FLOAT ON YOUR COFFEE WHEN YOU DUNK YOUR DOUGHNUTS?

© 1993 United Feature Syndicate, Inc.

YUCK! GARFIELD!

JIM DAVIS 6-29

© 1993 United Feature Syndicate, Inc.

DID YOU KNOW THE MAILMAN HAS BEEN WORKING OUT?

© 1993 United Feature Syndicate, Inc.

JIM DAVIS 7-16

WHAT ARE YOU DOING?

THANKS FOR RUINING IT FOR US

JIM DAVIS 7-17

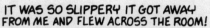

© 1993 United Feature Syndicate, Inc.

© 1993 United Feature Syndicate, Inc.

© 1993 United Feature Syndicate, Inc.

HAVE YOU NOTICED ONE OF ODIE'S EARS IS LONGER THAN THE OTHER?

© 1993 United Feature Syndicate, Inc.

© 1993 United Feature Syndicate, Inc.

UH, GARFIELD...

I'M STORING CHOCOLATE CHIP COOKIES FOR THE WINTER

YO DE LAY
HEE HOO

© 1993 United Feature Syndicate, Inc.

© 1993 United Feature Syndicate, Inc.

MY DATE IS VERY SOPHISTICATED, GARFIELD

AND SHE LIKES WITTY MEN

© 1993 United Feature Syndicate, Inc.

THIS FAKE FAUCET SHOULD CRACK HER UP

SUBTLE, YET DISGUSTING

JIM DAVIS 10-1

© 1993 United Feature Syndicate, Inc.

© 1993 United Feature Syndicate, Inc.

IT'S AMAZING WHAT ONE CAN DO WITH A ROLLING PIN

JIM DAVIS 10-13

OTHER GARFIELD BOOKS IN THIS SERIES

COLOUR TV SPECIALS

Here Comes Garfield	£2.95
Garfield On The Town	£2.95
Garfield In The Rough	£2.95
Garfield In Disguise	£2.95
Garfield In Paradise	£2.95
Garfield Goes To Hollywood	£2.95
A Garfield Christmas	£3.99
Garfield's Thanksgiving	£2.95
Garfield's Feline Fantasies	£2.95
Garfield Gets A Life	£2.95

GARFIELD GALLERIES

Gallery 1	£2.99
Gallery 2	£2.99
Gallery 3	£2.99
Gallery 5	£2.99
Gallery 7	£2.99

All Ravette books are available at your local bookshop or from the address below. Just tick the titles required and send the form with your remittance to:-

B.B.C.S., P.O. BOX 941, HULL, NORTH HUMBERSIDE HU1 3YQ
24 Hour Telephone Credit Card Line 01482 224626
Prices and availability are subject to change without notice.

Please enclose a cheque or postal order made payable to B.B.C.S. to the value of the cover price of the book and allow the following for postage and packing:

U.K. & B.F.P.O: £1.00 for the first book and 50p for each additional book to a maximum of £3.50.

Overseas & Eire: £2.00 for the first book, £1.00 for the second and 50p for each additional book.

BLOCK CAPITALS PLEASE

Name ....

Address ....

....

....

Cards accepted: Mastercard and Visa

Expiry Date........................... Signature...